Three Simple Rules

Three Simple Rules
A Wesleyan Way
of Living

Rueben P. Job

Abingdon Press
Nashville

Three Simple Rules

Copyright © 2007 by Abingdon Press

All rights reserved.

This book is printed on acid-free paper.

ISBN-13: 978-0-687-649662

13 14 15 16 17 18—18 17 16 15 14
Printed in the United States of America

Contents

"What then is the mark? Who is a Methodist, according to your own account?" I answer: A Methodist is one who has "the love of God shed abroad in his heart by the Holy Ghost given unto him;" one who "loves the Lord his God with all his heart, and with all his soul, and with all his mind, and with all his strength. God is the joy of his heart, and the desire of his soul; which is constantly crying out, "Whom have I in heaven but thee? and there is none upon earth that I desire beside thee! My God and my all! Thou art the strength of my heart, and my portion for ever!"

— "The Character of a Methodist," in *Works*, Vol. 8; page 341

Preface

THREE SIMPLE RULES
that will change your world

There are three simple rules that have the power to change the world. While they are ancient, they have seldom been fully put to the test. But when and where practiced, the world of things as they were was shaken until a new formation, a new world was formed. The Wesleyan movement is a prime example of this new creation that is formed when these three simple rules are adopted as a way of living.

We live in such a fast-paced, frenzied, and complex world that it is easy to believe we are all trapped into being someone we do not wish to be and living a life we do not desire to live. We long for some way to cut through the complexities and turbulence of everyday life. We search for a way to overcome the divisiveness that separates, disparages, disrespects, diminishes, and leaves us wounded and incomplete. We know deep within that the path we are on is not healthy or morally right and that it cannot lead to a positive ending. We fear that there is no way out.

The path we are on has become so well worn that only a radical change can jar us out of the deep ruts of our dilemma. And this radical change is possible because we see the devastating cost of going on as we are. Continuing on as we are is no longer a viable option. The risks are too high and the results too costly. But where are we to turn, what are we to do?

To seek help we turn to the One who created us, formed us, and loves us as we are and yet always seeks to lead us to become more than we are. When asked which commandment was most important, Jesus responded, " '... you shall love the Lord your God with all your heart, and with all your soul, and with all your mind, and with all your strength.' The second is this, 'You shall love your neighbor as yourself.' There is no other commandment greater than these" (Mark 12:29-31). Here we have the foundation and instruction for the faithful and good life in every age. It is both a simple and profound statement. It is easy to comprehend and challenging to attempt. And it remains a guide to the highest form of faithfulness and continues to hold the promise of a way of life that is both rewarding and fruitful in furthering God's kingdom on earth as it is in heaven.

We also turn to our roots and seek what it was in the past that enabled persons like us to live courageously and faithfully in their time. What was it that bound them to God and God's presence and power? What was it that bound them together in a common endeavor that challenged and transformed them into a holy and righteous movement? They needed and obviously found some instrument that, when used, brought them to a place of transformation.

I believe we have reached a place where, as a people of faith, we are ready to give serious consideration to another way, a more faithful way of living as disciples of Jesus Christ. This way must be so clear that it can be taught and practiced by everyone. It must be accessible and inviting to young and old, rich and poor, powerful and weak, and those of every theological persuasion. It is a large order, but we already have in our hands the blueprint for this way of living. And with God's help and our willingness, it can change our world.

This way of living was given to John Wesley in a time much like our own. He took this blueprint, fleshed it out, taught it, and practiced it. And now it has been passed on to us. Now it is up to us to see if we will take it, teach it, and practice it until it becomes our natural way of living—a way of living that will mark our life together and our lives as individual Christians. Some already practice this way of living, and I believe many more are ready to try it. I invite you to read the following pages to see if you are ready for this radical change of direction that is marked by these three simple rules:

1. Do No Harm
2. Do Good
3. Stay in Love With God

Rueben P. Job
Autumn 2007

Introduction

THE WORLD IN WHICH WE LIVE

Most of us never imagined we would be living in such a divided world. People of my age who lived through the Second World War were convinced that our world would be drawn together in harmony, peace, and plenty. The sacrifices made were so enormous that it seemed certain that we would never again permit our world to become so divided. But here we are in a world where divisions are growing deeper nearly every day. We had this naive expectation that we would just get better as we became educated and shared more of the world's riches. It looked like a natural and easy path to follow. Forgetting the struggles and sacrifices of the past may have led to a complacency that took community too lightly, individualism too seriously, and neglected our call to faithfulness to the gospel of Jesus Christ.

But alas, the world of peace and plenty for all has not happened. Nations are increasingly hostile toward one another; communities are divided around issues of education, development, and the status quo. Religion is divided with each claiming to have a firm grip on the truth. Denominations and congregations are divided over doctrine and what constitutes faithful discipleship and mortal sin. And families are divided by competing agendas, rival priorities, and the daily pressure to survive and thrive in an increasingly competitive culture.

I frequently receive mailings from denominational groups that appear to be intended not so much to nurture and heal as to divide and conquer. So often the rhetoric seems more like gossip than truth-telling in love, aimed at discovery and mutuality. The division, partisanship, and sharp criticism, not only of positions but also of persons, have not strengthened denominations, communities, congregations, families, or individuals. The louder our voices and the more strident our rhetoric, the weaker and more wounded we ourselves become. Our witness to the redeeming love of God loses its authenticity and its power as our unwillingness to be reconciled continues.

Those who seek to follow Jesus must be asking if this is the way Christians are to live. Are we really measuring up to our calling as children of God? Is there a better way for us to practice our faith? A way so simple and substantial that none are turned away and all are able to practice as together we engage in our quest for faithful living?

Are we the living answer to the prayer of Jesus, "Holy Father, protect them in your name that you have given me, so that they may be one, as we are one" (John 17:11b)? Do we look at one another and see movement toward our oneness in Christ? Do others look at us and see God at work in our life together? Is our way of living life-giving rather than life-draining? Is our way of living one that will enhance the quality of life of each of us for as long as we live?

At their best, Christians believe that the possibility of such a way of living exists and is open to all. When we have seen such a way of living practiced, we have not only been inspired by it but drawn to it. In our better moments we know we have not lived up to that shared belief of living the good and faithful life with Jesus Christ at the very center of all we do and are. Deep within, I believe all of us do want to live that faithful and fruitful life even though we have often turned away from God's invitation to holy living.

And we are not the first to struggle with faithfulness to the highest we know in Jesus Christ. The author of Colossians reminds the reader:

> As God's chosen ones, holy and beloved, clothe yourselves with compassion, kindness, humility, meekness, and patience. Bear with one another and, if anyone has a complaint against another, forgive each other; just as the Lord has forgiven you, so you also must forgive. Above all, clothe yourselves with love, which binds everything together in perfect harmony. (Colossians 3:12-14)

Here is clear reminder that the follower of Jesus Christ is God's chosen one and as such deserves and demands a certain way of living.

The text above is not unlike what one finds in Galatians 5, in which the ways of the world and the way of Christ are set in stark contrast. It reads,

By contrast, the fruit of the Spirit is love, joy, peace, patience, kindness, generosity, faithfulness, gentleness, and self-control.... If we live by the Spirit, let us also be guided by the Spirit. Let us not become conceited, competing against one another, envying one another. (5:22-26)

These admonitions were likely prompted by need for guidance in what faithful living meant in a world in which the way of Jesus was neither understood nor trusted. Controversy was the likely prompt that encouraged authors to put in writing the needed wisdom of Colossians and Galatians. They, like we, began their journey with Christ, determined to follow Jesus without straying or faltering from their commitment to follow him. Their world, like ours, was not on a path toward God and righteous living; and it was easy to stray and difficult to stay focused on Christ alone. The author of these texts knew that only a radical change could place the reader back on that road of faithfulness. A road that promises to take the faithful traveler ever nearer to God and God's chosen way for God's people.

Most of us yearn to live just such a good and faithful life in Christ. We do want to be faithful to the highest we know. We do want to practice our faith in ways that are healing and life-giving, not destructive and life-denying. Disagreement, dialogue, and debate are not foreign to Christians. We are not strangers to honest conversation, patience, loving acceptance, compromise, and mutual agreement. We are not strangers to forgiveness, conversion, transformation, reconciliation, and new life. And yet in recent years, it seems that these attributes have not been welcome guests or widely cultivated in our midst.

John Wesley anticipated times like these, and he knew that *everyone* needs help to live a holy and good life in a world like ours. He feared that new converts to Christ would fail to practice their faith and would, in his words, become more a "child of the devil" than before their conversion ("Journal from August 12, 1738, to November 1, 1739," in *Works*, Vol. 1; page 239).

He was fully aware that one could have all of the structures and systems right but could lose the

power of God that translates into a Christ-like life—
a way of holy living that is constantly reforming and
renewing the individual and the community. Because of these fears, Wesley was determined to fos-
ter the disciplined practices that would lead to
faithfulness to the way of Jesus. These practices were
outlined in the "General Rules," and instructions in
them and accountability to them was centered in the
classes that formed the United Societies of the early
Methodist movement (*The Book of Discipline of The
United Methodist Church—2004* (The United
Methodist Publishing House, 2004); ¶103).

It was these simple rules that transformed and
gave new life to women and men of high and low
estate, setting them on a path that would become a
movement that formed a denomination and transformed a forming nation in North America. We will
find quaint and dated some of the instructions
spelling out how the rules may be practiced. But the
three simple rules in themselves are contemporary
and exceptionally well suited to our time, our culture, and our needs today.

Do No Harm

"By doing no harm, by avoiding evil
of every kind, especially that which
is most generally practiced."
— *Discipline, 2004*; ¶103

Do No Harm

"If, however, you bite and devour one another, take care
that you are not consumed by one another."
(Galatians 5:15)

The first simple rule is "Do no harm." It is not that complicated. Even a child can understand what it means, and it is applicable to everyone at every stage of life. And when practiced, it works wonders in transforming the world around us. Most of us have observed and experienced the struggle to resolve complex and difficult issues. I have found that when this first simple rule was remembered, it often saved me from uttering a wrong word or considering a wrong response.

I have also found that this first simple step, when practiced, can provide a safe place to stand while the hard and faithful work of discernment is done. When we agree that we will not harm those with whom we disagree, conversation, dialogue, and discovery of new insight become possible. When our words and actions are guarded by this first simple rule, we have time and space to think about consequences before a word is spoken or an action taken.

Each of us knows of groups that are locked in conflict, sometimes over profound issues and sometimes over issues that are just plain silly. But the conflict is real, the divisions deep, and the consequences can often be devastating. If, however, all who are involved can agree to do no harm, the *climate* in which the conflict is going on is immediately changed. How is it changed? Well, if I am to do no harm, I can no longer *gossip* about the conflict. I can no longer *speak disparagingly* about those involved in the conflict. I can no longer *manipulate the facts* of the conflict. I can no longer *diminish* those who do not agree with me and must honor each as a child of God. *I will guard my lips, my mind and my heart so that my language will not disparage, injure or wound another child of God. I must do no harm, even while I seek a common good.*

> It may easily be believed, he who had this love in
> his heart would work no evil to his neighbour [sic].

It was impossible for him, knowingly and de-signedly, to do harm to any man. He was at the greatest distance from cruelty and wrong, from any unjust or unkind action. With the same care did he "set a watch before his mouth, and keep the door of his lips," lest he should offend in tongue, either against justice, or against mercy or truth. He put away All lying, falsehood and fraud; neither was guile found in his mouth. He spake evil of no man nor did an unkind word ever come out of his lips. ("Sermon 4, Scriptural Christianity," in *Works*, Vol. 5; page 41)

This act of disarming, laying aside our weapons and our desire to do harm, is revealing in other ways as well. We discover that we stand on common ground, inhabit a common and precious space, share a common faith, feast at a common table, and have an equal measure of God's unlimited love. When I am determined to do no harm to you, I lose my fear of you; and I am able to see you and hear you more clearly. Disarmed of the possibility to do harm, we find that good and solid place to stand where together we can seek the way forward in faithfulness to God.

When this first step is *not* taken, it usually is not because it is misunderstood or because it is too simple. More often it is a step not taken because it demands too much in the way of self-discipline and a very deep faith *that God will empower and lead the faithful.* To agree to take this first step is for many of us to agree with a theology and a practice too rigorous for our timid and tame commitment. If this step is so simple and so easily understood, why then do so many do so much harm? Because it is not an easy rule; and it does demand a *radical trust* in God's presence, power, wisdom, and guidance and a *radical obedience* to God's leadership. Practicing our faith in the world requires our deepest resolve, our greatest faith, our unwavering trust, and a very, very large measure of God's grace.

A second reason why this step is not taken may be that we have bound ourselves to a certain ideology or theology rather than binding ourselves to Jesus Christ as both Savior and Lord of all. We may have permitted our loyalty to a theological position to trump our loyalty to Jesus Christ. We may be so sure that "our way" is the right and only way that we cannot even consider that God's way could be different than our own. We have forgotten the importance of understanding clearly the God with whom we engage when we choose to follow the way of Jesus. To abandon the way of the world and follow the way of Jesus is a bold move and requires honest, careful, and prayerful consideration. It is not an inconsequential decision. Jesus himself told us to consider carefully the cost of discipleship: "For which of you, intending to build a tower, does not first sit down and estimate the cost, to see whether he has enough to complete it?. . . So therefore, none of you can become my disciple if you do not give up all your possessions" (Luke 14:28, 33).

To follow Jesus is to follow a God made known in Scripture, history, nature, our innermost self, and—most of all—in the life, death, and resurrection of Jesus of Nazareth. To follow Jesus is to follow One who fully trusts in God's goodness, love, and intimate involvement in the affairs of humankind. To follow this Jesus is to desire to be like him in our living and our dying. For some of us, that choice is just too frightening and too demanding; so we follow at a distance or turn away. But deep in the silence of our hearts, we know we do want to follow Jesus. We do know that following Jesus is the best and only way for us to live fully and faithfully. We really do know that it is the only way to live a peaceful, joyful, fruitful life. Deep in our hearts we know that this is the life we want. We do want to follow Jesus, even if it means giving up our favorite position or our favorite possession; and so we pray for grace to be faithful as we say yes to the invitation to faithfulness.

There may be another reason why we overlook this basic building block of Christian living—we are afraid of its consequences. To abandon the ways of the world for the way of Jesus is a radical step. While this step is very simple and easily understood, it is not easily achieved. We realize it may lead us where we do not wish to go. Are we really ready to give up political power for the power of God's love? Are we ready to give up our most cherished possession— the certainty that we are right and others wrong? Can we trust God enough to follow the ways of the

Spirit rather than the ways of the world? If we choose to follow this way, will we be seen as weak and at the mercy of others rather than as powerful and in control of every situation? If we choose this way, will our position be eroded and our point lost? The risk seems so great and often our fears speak so much louder than our faith.

Is it possible to live in this complex and violent world *without* doing harm? Are we supposed to turn the other cheek to those who distort the truth by selective use of the facts of any given situation? Is it wise to do no harm to those who seek to harm us, our future, or our reputation? Are we able to limit our response to a way that is not destructive to those who use false and violent words that seek to harm and destroy us? Is it possible to speak the truth in love and gentleness when others seem to speak partial truth in anger and hatred?

It is a challenging path to walk. Yet, even a casual reading of the gospel suggests that Jesus taught and practiced a way of living that did no harm. His life, his way of life, and his teaching demonstrated so well this first simple rule. And rather than inventing something new, John Wesley picked up on what Jesus taught and incorporated it into his structure for faithful living:

> Keep close, I beseech you, to every means of grace. Strive to walk in all the ordinances and commandments of God blameless ... "Add to your faith virtue; to virtue knowledge; to knowledge temperance; to temperance patience; to patience godliness; to godliness ... kindness; to ... kindness charity." ("Journal from May 6, 1760, to October 28, 1762," in *Works*, Vol. 3; page 88)

There are many reasons why we find it difficult to embrace the first of these three simple rules. But the good news is that we don't have to make this journey alone. There is *always* One who stands there with us. And not only stands there but invades us with Spirit Presence and Power to practice our faith with integrity and in fidelity to the One we seek to follow. This truth is at the heart of the Incarnation and of Pentecost. The good news is that it is possible to practice a way of living that is in harmony with the life of Jesus and survive, even thrive, in a world like ours. It is both a challenging and rewarding way to live; and each of us, with God's help, can live such a life fully, faithfully, and joyfully.

Wesley said that to continue on the way of salvation, that is living in harmony with God, we should begin "by doing no harm, by avoiding evil of every kind, especially that which is most generally practiced" (*Discipline, 2004*; ¶103). But Wesley was not alone in his insight about this essential element of any faithful response to Jesus Christ.

Thomas á Kempis in *The Imitation of Christ* shows great concern about the ease with which we slip into sinful response in our relationships with others. In his translation of this classic book, William C. Creasy interprets the author's concern as follows:

> We cannot trust ourselves too much, because we often lack grace and understanding. The light within us is small, and we soon let even this burn out for lack of care. Moreover, we often fail to notice how inwardly blind we are; for example, we frequently do wrong, and to make

matters worse, we make excuses about it! Sometimes we are moved by passion and think it zeal. We condemn small things in others and pass over serious things in ourselves. We are quick enough to feel it when others hurt us—and we even harbor those feelings—but we do not notice how much we hurt others. A person who honestly examines his own behavior would never judge other people harshly. (*The Imitation of Christ: A Timeless Classic for Contemporary Readers* (Ave Maria Press, Inc., 2004); page 69)

What would it mean if we took this first simple rule seriously? First of all, it would mean an examination of the way we live and practice our faith. And if this examination were thorough, it would surely lead to a change in the way we practice our faith. To do no harm is a proactive response to all that is evil—all that is damaging and destructive to humankind and God's good creation, and therefore, ultimately destructive to us. To adopt this first simple rule as our own is a giant step toward transforming the world in which we live.

To do no harm means that I will be on guard so that all my actions and even my silence will not add injury to another of God's children or to any part of God's creation. As did John Wesley and those in the early Methodist movement before me, I too will determine every day that my life will always be invested in the effort to bring healing instead of hurt; wholeness instead of division; and harmony with the ways of Jesus rather than with the ways of the world. When I commit myself to this way, I must see each person as a child of God—a recipient of love unearned, unlimited, and undeserved—just like myself. And it is this vision of every other person as the object of God's love and deep awareness that I too live in that loving Presence that can hold me accountable to my commitment to do no harm.

Perhaps the greatest consequence of all is that we are formed and transformed to live more and more as Jesus lived. And this personal transformation leads to transformation of the world around us as well. As two people in a long and successful marriage begin to think, act, and even look like each other, so those who practice this simple rule begin to think, act, and perhaps even look like Jesus. It is a gigantic step toward living the holy life that brings healing and goodness to all it touches. This simple step will change your life in good and wonderful ways, but there is more.

Do Good

"By doing good; by being in every kind merciful after their power; as they have opportunity, doing good of every possible sort, and, as far as possible, to all. . . ."
— *Discipline, 2004*; ¶103

Do Good

"Whoever does good is from God." (3 John 11b)

"God anointed Jesus of Nazareth with the Holy Spirit and with power; how he went about doing good . . . "
(Acts 10:38)

"You owe your conscience to God; to one another you owe nothing but mutual love." (*Letters of Saint Augustine,*
trans. John Leinenweber (Triumph, 1992); page 182)

There is scarce any possible way of doing good, for which here is not daily occasion. . . . Here are poor families to be relieved: Here are children to be educated: Here are workhouses, wherein both young and old gladly receive the word of exhortation: Here are the prisons, and therein a complication of all human wants. ("Journal from August 12, 1738, to November 1, 1739," in *Works,* Vol. 1; page 181)

Now things begin to get even more complicated. Just when we thought we were ready to buy into the idea of not doing harm to anyone or anything, we are faced with an even more difficult choice. Once again, we remember the words of Jesus, "But I say to you that listen, Love your enemies, do good to those who hate you, bless those who curse you, pray for those who abuse you" (Luke 6:27-28). To do good is a serious challenge from Wesley and a direct command from Jesus. But what does it mean for me to "do good"? It does sound simple, but where do I begin? What are the boundaries, the limits? Is this simple admonition too difficult for me? What does it mean? What does doing good look like in our divided, hostile, and wounded world?

We are not the first to ask the question. Wesley was confronted with the same challenge and he found a reasonable way to respond:

> . . . this commandment is written in his heart, "That he who loveth God, love his brother also." And he accordingly loves his neighbour [sic] as himself; he loves every man as his own soul. His heart is full of love to all mankind, to every child of "the Father of the spirits of all flesh." That a man is not personally known to him, is no bar to

his love; no, nor that he is known to be such as he approves not, that he repays hatred for his good-will. For he "loves his enemies;" yea, and the enemies of God, "the evil and the unthankful." And if it be not in his power to "do good to them that hate him," yet he ceases not to pray for them.... ("The Character of a Methodist," in *Works*, Vol.8, page 343)

The words of Jesus and of Wesley suggest that doing good is a universal command. That is, doing good is not limited to those like me or those who like me. Doing good is directed at everyone, even those who do not fit my category of "worthy" to receive any good that I or others can direct their way. This command is also universal in that no one is exempt from it.

Doing good, like doing no harm, is a proactive way of living. I do not need to wait to be asked to do some good deed or provide some needed help. I do not need to wait until circumstances cry out for aid to relieve suffering or correct some horrible injustice. I can decide that my way of living will come down on the side of doing good to all in every circumstance and in every way I can. I can decide that I will choose a way of living that nourishes goodness and strengthens community.

This way of living will require a careful and continual assessment of my life and the world in which I live. It will require an even more bold and radical step than not doing harm to those who may disagree with me and even seek to harm me. For now I am committing myself to seeking good for everyone in my world and everyone in God's world. Even those little offenses, like cutting in ahead of me in traffic, to the large offenses, such as considering me less than a child of God, can never move me outside the circle of goodness that flows from God to me and through me to the world. Every act and every word must pass through the love and will of God and there be measured to discover if its purpose does indeed bring good and goodness to all it touches.

Now, I am willing to do a little good, maybe even give another couple of hundred dollars to my congregation, and now and then give a contribution to Habitat for Humanity, or the local food bank; but tell me, where are the boundaries? Will the demands for my time, my influence, and my money become overwhelming? Even I can see that this could quickly get out of hand and, before I know it, my whole life is given away. I am not sure I am willing to live in such an uncontrolled situation. Perhaps *control* is the dominant word here.

There are obstacles to this way of living, and at the top of the list may be my desire to be in control. I like to know where I am going, and I like to know what it will cost to get there. That is why doing all the good I can is such a frightening idea. The needs of the world, my community, my congregation, my family are so great that if I were to do all the good I could, I might feel compelled to give everything away for some good cause. Would that be the right thing to do? Even if it were the right thing to do, could I do it? I already have too many responsibilities, too many commitments, and too many others who depend upon me.

Or, what if I offer my gift of goodness, small or large, and it is rejected? Suppose I were to seek compromise in conflict and my efforts were ridiculed?

What if my efforts were seen as weakness and my concerns were overlooked? What if my gift of goodness was accepted and then misused in ways that were abhorrent to me?

> You have heard that it was said, "You shall love your neighbor and hate your enemy." But I say to you, Love your enemies and pray for those who persecute you, so that you may be children of your Father in heaven; for he makes his sun rise on the evil and on the good, and sends rain on the righteous and on the unrighteous. (Matthew 5:43-45)

The truth is that my gift of goodness may be rejected, ridiculed, and misused. But my desire to do good is not limited by the thoughts or actions of others. My desire to do good is in response to God's invitation to follow Jesus, and it *is in my control.* I can determine to extend hospitality and goodness to all I meet. I can decide to do good to all, even to those who disagree with me and turn against what I believe is right and good. And the reward for my doing good is not cancelled or diminished by the response to my acts of goodness. I will have the reward of knowing I did what was right and pleasing to God. I will still be identified, known, and loved as a child of God. What could be a greater reward than this?

It is true that these three rules are simple and easy to understand. We almost always know when our words or actions do harm and when they do good. And deep within us are both the desire and the nudging voice of the Spirit, telling us to fashion and maintain a living and life-giving relationship with God. Yes, the rules are *simple* and they are *easily understood*. But that does not make them *easy to practice*. Wesley frequently examined his own life to see if he was living in harmony with these three simple rules that he taught.

This, however, with a sentence in the Evening Lesson, put me upon considering my own state more deeply. And what then occurred to me was as follows: . . . His judgment concerning holiness is new. He no longer judges it to be an outward thing: To consist either in doing no harm, in doing good, or in using the ordinances of God. He sees it is the life of God in the soul; the image of God fresh stamped on the heart; an entire renewal of the mind in every temper and thought, after the likeness of Him that created it. ("Journal from August 12, 1738, to November 1, 1739," in *Works*, Vol. 1; page 161)

The "image of God fresh stamped on the heart" is the ultimate reward of faithfulness, and it will certainly lead me to the decision to do all the good I can for everyone I can. For it is God who loves all and permits the rain to fall on all. So, this decision will mean that I must seek good for all. I must seek what is best for those whose position and condition may be far different than my vision for them. It will mean that I will seek to heal the wounds of my sisters and brothers, no matter if their social position, economic condition, educational achievement, or lifestyle is radically different from mine. It will mean that the words and acts that wound and divide will be changed to words and acts that heal and bring together. It will mean that movements that seek to divide and conquer will become movements that seek to unite and empower all. It will mean that the common good will be my first thought and what is good for me will become a secondary thought.

Of course, this is a challenging way to live. To love God with my whole being and to love my neighbor as much as I love myself was never declared to be easy; but it was declared to be essential to our spiritual life, our life of faith, and our life with God. The three rules are simple; but when I look at this simple and practical step to a transformed world, I begin to see how complicated and costly living with Jesus can become.

Jesus identified himself as "one who serves" (Luke 22:27). Paul said, "Let love be genuine; hate what is evil, hold fast to what is good; love one another . . . outdo one another in showing honor. . . . Contribute to the needs of the saints; extend hospitality to strangers" (Romans 12:9-10, 13). It is not difficult to see how revolutionary the words and lifestyle of Jesus and the early Christians must have seemed to themselves and to the world in which they lived.

Their way of living was a radical departure from the accepted practices of the powerful and the weak. To walk with Jesus meant to focus on something larger than the individual and Someone larger than any human being or human institution. And that is exactly what it means today!

> His servant I am, and, as such, am employed according to the plain direction of his word, "As I have opportunity, doing good unto all men:" And his providence clearly concurs with his word; which has disengaged me from all things else, that I might singly attend on this very thing, "and go about doing good." ("Journal from August 12, 1738, to November 1, 1739," in *Works*, Vol. 1; page 202)

To singly attend to doing good is a simple rule, but it is also unbelievably challenging. But wait a minute. What if I forget about myself? It is an incredible idea but one that Jesus seemed to like a lot. What if I really did think about and put God first in my life? What if I did think of the needs of others first? What if I permitted what is good for the community to be my guide rather than my own personal needs? Would this bring me nearer to what Wesley had in mind? What Jesus had in mind? I have a feeling that it would.

However, it would also expose us to the danger that some destructive ways could overtake us once again. There was a time when we were told to forget ourselves, deny ourselves, be humble, and accept a low opinion of ourselves. While this may have tempered our rush toward arrogance and selfishness, it also proved to be self-destructive and not even good for the larger community. There is such a thing as *healthy self-denial.* It is what Jesus asks of us. And there is such a thing as *unhealthy self-denial,* which people, institutions, and movements gone astray from the way of Jesus often lead us into. Unfortunately, in trying to avoid unhealthy self-denial we often make a giant leap from a healthy self-denial to an unhealthy self-worship as promoted by our culture.

It is our culture that reminds me that I have become the most important person in the world and therefore I must take care of myself *first.* Of course, the purpose of this campaign is not my well-being but the marketing of some product. Nevermind the needs of others, take care of yourself first. So, our culture has created a climate where corporate executives rob shareholders and plunge employees into poverty. A culture in which this world's treasures are rapidly gravitating away from those who desperately need a reasonable share of those treasures to survive. A culture in which anything goes as long as it is to my advantage—and I don't get caught. A climate in which it has become easy to turn away from the social and economic injustice that does immense harm to many and provides rich benefits to few. We live in a culture that tends to be destructive to the very self worth and dignity of every child of God. Far too many times we have contributed to a competitive culture that encourages greed and selfishness and discourages compassion, sharing, fairness, and commitment to the common good.

But taking appropriate care of self and living selflessly are not opposites. Rather they are each essential elements of a healthy and productive life. To love God with all of life and to love neighbor as self is not to denigrate, deny, or devalue self. It is to proclaim the heart of our theology as Christians and to place enormous value on self and on neighbor. It is to choose to live in the reign of God NOW. To begin to live as a citizen of a new order in which God's love for all creation is recognized and proclaimed in word and deed.

Living in this new way never suggests that self-care is unimportant or unnecessary. Loving oneself does demand caring for oneself in a culture and in systems that are often destructive to self. And that self-care begins with the acknowledgement and reminder that each one of us is the object of God's love. Each one of us is embraced in the unlimited, saving, and transforming love of God. Each one of us is the "apple of [God's] eye" and is always and ultimately safe in the strong arms of God (Zechariah 2:8). When this knowledge is deeply imbedded within, we are better able to see the distinction between denying self and caring for self. This knowledge of my true self can free me from having to control everything and can place me on a path of greater trust in God and greater capacity to live fully and faithfully. Would it free me to do good, all the good I can? I have a feeling it would be a good place to begin. It is another simple step that will make a huge difference in transforming our world.

These first two rules are important and bring immediate results; but without the third rule, the first two become increasingly impossible. Staying in love with God is the foundation to all of life. It is in a vital relationship with God that we are enlivened, sustained, guided, called, sent, formed, and transformed. The writer of the Psalm 127 declared, "Unless the LORD builds the house, those who build it labor in vain" (verse 1a). We practice the rules, but God sends the power that enables us to keep them. We practice the rules; but God does the transforming, the renewing, and the building of the house—the house of our lives, the house of our church, and the house of our world.

While these first two rules are essential, the truth is, we cannot fix on our own much of what ails us. Legislation or committees will not solve our divisiveness, our woundedness, or our brokenness. The clarity we seek on a multitude of issues and the faithfulness and fruitfulness we long for cannot be manufactured on our own. Only living in the healing, loving, redeeming, forming, and guiding light and presence of God will bring the redemption, healing, transformation, and guidance that is so desperately needed. That is why staying in love with God is the essential third simple rule.

Stay in Love With God

"By attending upon all the ordinances
of God. . . ."
— *Discipline, 2004*; ¶103

Stay in Love With God

"Seek the LORD and his strength; seek his presence continually." (Psalm 105:4)

"As you therefore have received Christ Jesus the Lord, continue to live your lives in him, rooted and built up in him and established in the faith, just as you were taught, abounding in thanksgiving." (Colossians 2:6-7)

Ordinance is a strange word to our ears. But to John Wesley, it was a word that described the practices that kept the relationship between God and humans vital, alive, and growing. He names public worship of God, the Lord's Supper, private and family prayer, searching the Scriptures, Bible study, and fasting as essential to a faithful life. While we may have different names for our essential spiritual disciplines, these practices can become a life-giving source of strength and guidance for us. Wesley saw these disciplines as central to any life of faithfulness to God in Christ. He saw that the consistent practice of these spiritual disciplines kept those who sought to follow Christ in touch with the presence and power of Christ so they could fulfill their desire to live as faithful disciples.

Spiritual disciplines teach us to live our lives in harmony with something larger than ourselves and larger than that which the world values as ultimate. In her book, *Illuminated Life*, Joan Chittister puts it this way, "All we have in life is life. Things—the cars, the houses, the educations, the jobs, the money— come and go, turn to dust between our fingers, change and disappear. . . . the secret of life . . . is that it must be developed from the inside out" (Orbis Books, 2000; page 14).

Living in the presence of and in harmony with the living God who is made known in Jesus Christ and companions us in the Holy Spirit is to live life from the inside out. It is to find our moral direction, our wisdom, our courage, our strength to live faithfully from the One who authored us, called us, sustains us, and sends us into the world as witnesses who daily practice the way of living with Jesus. Spiritual disciplines keep us in that healing, re-deeming presence and power of God that forms and transforms each of us more and more into the image of the One we seek to follow.

We may name our spiritual disciplines differently, but we too must find our way of living and practicing those disciplines that will keep us in love with God—practices that will help keep us positioned in such a way that we may hear and be responsive to God's slightest whisper of direction and receive God's promised presence and power every day and in every situation. It is in these practices that we learn to hear and respond to God's direction. It is in these practices that we learn to trust God as revealed in Jesus Christ. It is in these practices that we learn of God's love for us. It is where our love for God is nurtured and sustained. Incorporating these practices in our way of living will keep us in love with God and assure us of God's love for us in this world and the world to come.

This simple rule will be constructed differently for each of us because each of us is unique. But there are some common essentials for all of us, such as a daily time of prayer; reflection upon and study of Scripture; regular participation in the life of a

Christian community, including weekly worship and regular participation in the Lord's Supper; doing some act of goodness or mercy; and taking opportunities to share with and learn from others who also seek to follow the way of Jesus. It is through these practices that we find the courage, strength, and direction to walk faithfully and with integrity in the way of Jesus.

We can accuse Jesus of many things, but we cannot accuse him of neglecting his relationship with God. He must have learned early how important it was to stay close to God if he was to fulfill his mission in the world. He must have learned early that there was power available to live the faithful, the fruitful, the good life and that this power involved staying connected, staying in touch, and staying in love with his trusted Abba (Mark 14:36; Romans 8:15). He found not only his strength and guidance but his greatest joy in communion, companionship with his loving Abba. Perhaps it was these experiences that prompted his teaching about prayer and faithfulness and probably gave birth to his question to Peter.

Look at Jesus. The world did not pay any attention to him. He was crucified and put away. His message of love was rejected by a world in search of power, efficiency, and control. But there he was, appearing with wounds in his glorified body to a few friends who had eyes to see, ears to hear, and hearts to understand. This rejected, unknown, wounded Jesus simply asked, "Do you love me, do you really love me?" He whose only concern had been to announce the unconditional love of God had only one question to ask, "Do you love me?" (*In the Name of Jesus*, by Henri J. M. Nouwen (Crossroad, 1989); pages 36–37)

The question Jesus asked of Peter in John 21:15ff, "Do you love me?" reveals a great deal about the essentials of our relationship with God. Three times Jesus asked, "Do you love me?" and three times Peter answered in the affirmative. Staying in love with God was the primary issue of a faithful life then, and it is today. For from such a life of love for God will flow the goodness and love of God to the world. It can be no other way. One who is deeply in love will be constantly formed and transformed by that relationship. And such a transformed life will be a natural channel of God's goodness, power, and presence in the world.

Therefore, each time Jesus raised the question, "Do you love me?" he also declared how Peter and the world would know if he was obedient to God. Holy living will not be discovered, achieved, continued, and sustained without staying in love with God. And while staying in love with God involves prayer, worship, study, and the Lord's Supper, it also involves feeding the lambs, tending the sheep, and providing for the needs of others (John 21:15-16). Feeding the lambs and tending the sheep are the signs of love that we exchange with God. And they are signs of the love that the world can understand. Spiritual disciplines not only include practices that bind us to God every day but they also include actions that heal the pain, injustice, and inequality of our world. It is impossible to stay in love with God and not desire to see God's goodness and grace shared with the entire world.

What makes the temptation of power so seemingly irresistible? Maybe it is that power offers an easy substitute for the hard task of love. It seems easier to be God than to love God, easier to control people than to love people, easier to own life than to love life. Jesus asks, "Do you love me?" We ask, "Can we sit at your right hand and your left hand in your Kingdom?" (Nouwen; page 77)

The fact that Jesus asked Peter three times if he loved him is a very revealing exchange. Peter denied Jesus three times (Matthew 26:75), but here he declared his love three times. Peter was drawn toward a new beginning, a new future. The failures of the past are to be forgotten and the new possibilities are to be embraced. And those new possibilities are reflected in the mission given to Peter.

Each of us has our own litany of failures to recite, but the good news is that we can start again. We can also recite the failures of institutions and systems that are near and dear to us. The good news is that the past can be forgiven. God does offer another chance to people like Peter, whose denial seemed like such an enormous failure, and to each of us, no matter what our failures may have been. The question to Peter becomes the question to each of us, "Do you love me?" When we respond in the affirmative, the response from God is always the same, "Feed my lambs, tend my sheep."

Earlier, Jesus directed the disciples to an astounding, boat swamping catch of fish and then invites them all to breakfast on the beach. It was after this lavish display of grace, goodness, and love that Peter was offered opportunity to declare his love and make a new beginning of faithfulness. As Peter declared his love, Jesus gave some insight about what was to come to this faithful disciple:

"Very truly, I tell you, when you were younger, you used to fasten your own belt and to go wherever you wished. But when you grow old, you will stretch out your hands, and someone else will fasten a belt around you and take you where you do not wish to go." (He said this to indicate the kind of death by which he would glorify

God.) After this he said to him, "Follow me."
(John 21:18-19)

Not all of the disciples became martyrs, but all
were very likely taken places that they had not intended to go. When we say yes to God's call of love,
we are released from so many things; and our free-
dom in Christ is a wonderful gift to be enjoyed. But
we too will likely be led to places we had not intended to go. Disciples of Jesus do have great free-
dom in Christ, and they also have great loyalty to
the way of Christ. Consequently, they are often
called to action and restraint as they stay in love with
God and seek to live a life of faithfulness, fidelity,
and integrity.

The pages you have read promise a way of living
to change your world. Three simple rules that can
be easily understood and practiced by everyone
every day of their lives are the focus of this way of
living. It's a way of living that can guard your life
from doing evil and enable you to do good. A way
of living that provides a way to stay in love with
God in this world and the next. A way of living that

promises a way to claim and enjoy your full inheritance as children of God. Sounds almost too good to be true, doesn't it? But the facts are that those who have followed these three simple rules have discovered their world changed and they were enabled to claim their full inheritance as children of God.

Of course it would be foolish to assume we will escape what the first disciples could not avoid. There will be hardships, there will temptations to fall back into the ways of the kingdoms of this world. There may be times when we, as the disciples before us, stumble and fall into doing foolish things like squabbling about who will be first among us. But the good news is we can rise above our denials of the way of Jesus, receive forgiveness, and begin again our life of fidelity and faithfulness to God in Christ. Will you begin today the practice of these three simple rules?

The rules are simple, but the way is not easy. Only those with great courage will attempt it, and only those with great faith will be able to walk this exciting and demanding way. There are many other options for us to choose, but they are all lesser options and lead to lesser results that range from poor to disastrous. The question from Jesus continues for each of us, "My daughter, my son, do you love me?" And of course there is only one answer that we want to give, "Yes Lord, you know everything, you know that I love you." The next question then becomes, are we ready to choose the costly way that involves these three simple rules as our way of living? I believe many are ready to make that high and holy choice today, and I shall always pray that I and all who read these pages will make that choice new every morning.

A Guide for Daily Prayer

O begin! Fix some part of every day for private exercises. You may acquire the taste which you have not: What is tedious at first, will afterwards be pleasant. Whether you like it or no, read and pray daily. It is for your life; there is no other way. . . . Do justice to your own soul; give it time and means to grow. Do not starve yourself any longer. Take up your cross, and be a Christian altogether. Then will all the children of God rejoice. . . . ("Letters to Mr. John Trembath," in *Works*, Vol. 12; page 254)

Prayer is at the center of a transformed life. This Wesleyan way of living is inconceivable and impossible without a regular and disciplined practice of prayer. Such a disciplined life of prayer will be as diverse and as distinct as our fingerprint. For some it will mean the formal language of prayer, for others the quiet listening in God's presence; but for all it will be a turning Godward in response to God's invitation to a relationship that is eternal and immediate at the same time.

I have a friend who describes his life of prayer as "staying in touch with the home office." I have other friends who describe their prayer lives as mostly verbal or mostly reading and responding to Scripture, others who seek ways to fulfill the biblical call to "pray without ceasing" (1 Thessalonians 5:17), and still others who make the ancient liturgy and prayers of the church their own.

And yet, within all of this diversity there is a unifying constant. That unifying constant is a movement toward God that results in transformation of life and how life is valued and lived out in the everyday experiences of our existence. It is this transformed and transforming way of living, this strengthening of the bond that binds us to God, that we seek as we follow the three simple rules offered by John Wesley to the early Methodist movement and now to us.

To remind us and assist us in the daily practice of prayer, I have included a brief liturgy outline for the beginning, middle, and end of the day. Each brief liturgy includes several movements that contribute to a life of prayer. I invite you to incorporate these simple practices into your daily schedule. The time given and the content included in each movement of prayer are entirely in your hands. Some will choose different Scripture passages from a lectionary and prayers that have been passed on to us from others. The important thing is that the Scripture and prayers speak to you and keep you aware of and in touch with God's presence every day.

There are many ways of prayer, and there is no special merit in this pattern of prayer that I have proposed. You may already have a well-established pattern of prayer that keeps your relationship with God vital and alive. You may already practice a way of prayer that yields the fruit of transformation in your life and in your way of living. If so, by all means continue what you are already doing as you make Wesley's three simple rules your own. If you do not have such a pattern of prayer, I invite you to make the pattern suggested here a place of beginning until your own pattern of prayer becomes a way of living that keeps you bound to God with the bonds of love, faith, and radical trust.

Prayer at the Beginning of the Day

Loving Teacher, come and make your home in our hearts this day. Dwell within us all day long and save us from error or foolish ways. Teach us today to do no harm, to do good, and assist us so that we may stay in loving relationship with you and our neighbor. Help us today to be an answer to another's prayer so that we may be one of your signs of hope in the world you love.

SCRIPTURE

"You show me the path of life.

In your presence there is fullness of joy;

in your right hand are pleasures forevermore" (Psalm 16:11).

You may wish to choose a different passage for each day's reflection. *A Guide to Prayer for All Who Seek God* (Upper Room, 2006) and *This Day: A Wesleyan Way of Prayer* (Abingdon, 2004) are two sources for daily Scripture readings.

REFLECTION

Consider the meaning of the Scripture passage for your life this day. Pay attention to any response that is prompted by the text you have chosen to read.

PRAYER

A time for prayers of thanksgiving and petition as you begin your day.

OFFERING

"Here am I, the servant of the Lord; let it be with me according to your word" (Luke 1:38). Offering ourselves to God to be used this day as God chooses.

GOD'S PROMISE

"And remember, I am with you always, to the end of the age" (Matthew 28:20b).

Prayer at Midday

God of love, holiness, and strength, we thank you for the gift of your presence through the morning hours. Continue to make yourself and your way known to us throughout the remaining hours of the day. Grant us grace to follow you in faithfulness, joy, and peace. We are yours.

SILENCE

"Speak, LORD, for your servant is listening" (1 Samuel 3:9). Listening for God's direction as we wait for guidance and direction for the remaining hours of the day.

RESPONSE

"'It is the LORD; let him do what seems good to him'" (1 Samuel 3:18b).

PRAYER

Responding with gratitude for God's grace and direction promised and already experienced this day.

BLESSING

"My soul clings to you;
 your right hand upholds me" (Psalm 63:8).

Prayer at the End of the Day

Inviting God's Activity

Tender shepherd of my soul; make yourself and your way known to me in this evening time of prayer and reflection. Bring awareness of my failures and confidence in your desire and ability to forgive my sins, heal my wounds, and mend my broken places. By the power of your presence bring me to the end of the day whole, complete, and at peace with you, my neighbor and myself. Grant a night of peaceful rest and send me forth tomorrow as a witness to your love and grace.

A Continuing Request

"Create in me a clean heart, O God,
    and put a new and right spirit within me.
Do not cast me away from your presence,
    and do not take your holy spirit from me.
Restore to me the joy of your salvation" (Psalm 51:10-12a).

SCRIPTURE

"Protect me, O God, for in you I take refuge.
I say to the LORD, 'You are my Lord;
  I have no good apart from you'" (Psalm 16:1-2).

GATHERING THE DAY

Remembering

A time of reflection on the day's experiences. Note the positive and the negative experiences and ask, "How have I contributed to each? What is God saying to me through the events of this day?"

Confessing

A time of owning up to our own weakness, failure, and sin.

Forgiving

A time of asking for and accepting God's forgiveness, and a time of offering forgiveness to ourselves and to all who may have injured us or those we love.

Thanksgiving

Give thanks for each of the gifts of life that God has granted this day.

OFFERING

"I do here covenant with you, O Christ,
    to take my lot with you as it may fall.
Through your grace I promise
    that neither life nor death shall part me from you"
("Wesley's Covenant Service," in *The United Methodist Book of Worship* (The United Methodist Publishing House, 1992); page 293).

BLESSING

Forgiven, free from sin and the burdens of life, receive the peace of Christ for a restful and refreshing night, embraced in the everlasting arms of God.

"I will both lie down and sleep in peace;
    for you alone, O LORD, make me lie down in
        safety" (Psalm 4:8).

These are the General Rules of our Societies; all of which we are taught of God to observe, even in his written Word, which is the only rule, and the sufficient rule, both of our faith and practice. And all of these we know his Spirit writes on our truly awakened hearts.

— *Discipline, 2004;* ¶ 103

Stay in Love With God

Do no   harm   by an - y word or   deed;   do

good   wher - ev - er there is   need.   Re -

main   at - ten - tive to God's word.   Stay in love with

God,   stay in love with   God.

Words: Adapted from John Wesley
Music: Raquel Mora Martinez
© 2007 Abingdon Press